By Jim Kerr

CONTENTS

INTRODUCTION

Cricket is a bat-and-ball sport played between two teams of eleven players. The game was first played in England several hundred years ago and is now one of the most popular sports in the world. Although it is widely played, the best teams in the world (known as the Test-playing nations) are from places as diverse as England, Australia, India, Sri Lanka, Zimbabwe, South Africa, Bangladesh, New Zealand, Pakistan and the West Indies.

GUIDE TO SYMBOLS & ARROWS

*To help you understand movement and direction
we have used the following:*

**The red arrows indicate the swing
of the bat.**

**The yellow arrows indicate the
direction of the ball.**

THE PITCH

It is possible to organise an informal game of cricket in any park or playground. You'll need a bat, a tennis ball and a set of stumps. A proper match, played with a hard ball, will need to take place on a cricket pitch with two sets of stumps.

BOUNDARY

This marks the edge of the playing area. On a proper cricket ground, it is marked with a continuous white line or rope that is oval in shape. In a park game, it may be marked by cones placed in a large circle. The ball is in play when it is inside the boundary. Once a ball (or player) falls outside the boundary, it is out of play.

OUTFIELD

This is the area of a cricket field between the square and the boundary.

INFIELD

This is the area of a cricket field closer to the pitch.

THE SQUARE

This is the area of a cricket field on which the pitch is prepared by ground staff. They mow the grass very short.

THE PITCH

This is where the game takes place. It is a strip of mown grass that has been flattened with a heavy roller and prepared by ground staff. A cricket pitch is 22 yards (20 m) in length. It is also called the wicket.

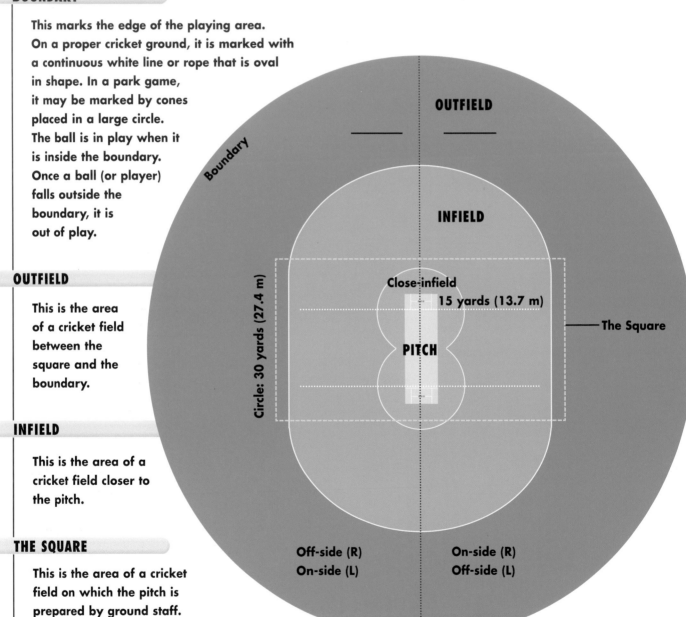

THE CREASE

The crease is marked out with white lines at each end of a cricket pitch. It marks the area in which a bowler may place their feet and where a batsman must stand. The bowling crease is the line along which the stumps are placed. The popping crease is parallel to the bowling crease. A batsman must ground their bat behind this line when making a run. The return crease is drawn at right angles from each end of the bowling crease.

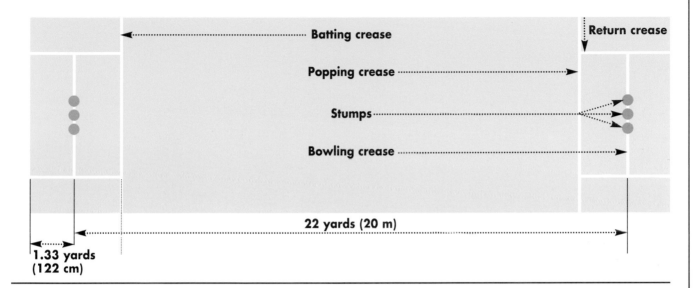

Batting crease

Return crease

Popping crease

Stumps

Bowling crease

22 yards (20 m)

1.33 yards (122 cm)

Three stumps are placed into the ground at each end of a cricket pitch.

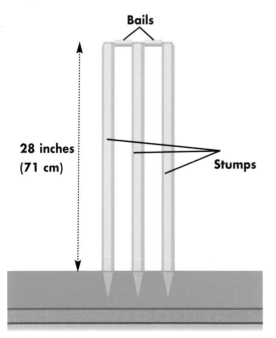

Bails

28 inches (71 cm)

Stumps

The three stumps are leg stump, middle stump and off stump. The stump nearest the batsman is the leg stump.

THE STUMPS

Stumps are 28 inches (71 cm) in height from the ground to the top of the stump. The total width of the stumps is nine inches (23 cm). They should be placed near enough together, so the ball cannot pass between any two stumps. Two bails are placed on top of each set of stumps.

UMPIRES

Cricket umpires are in charge of starting and finishing an organised match and enforcing the rules of play. They make important decisions during the course of a game, for example deciding whether a batsman is out. Umpires stand either behind the stumps or in the square leg position (see page 6).

SCORERS

Both teams have a scorer, who must keep an accurate record of match statistics in a scorecard or book. The scorers sit together outside the field of play and must observe and acknowledge signals from the umpires.

THE FIELD

The captain will set the field, sometimes after talking with the bowler. When you are asked to field in a particular position, it is important that you know what part of the field you are patrolling, and what your role and responsibilities are. General fielding skills are covered on pages 36 to 41.

FIELDING POSITIONS

This diagram shows most of the possible fielding positions for a right-handed batsman. Only some will be used at any one time.

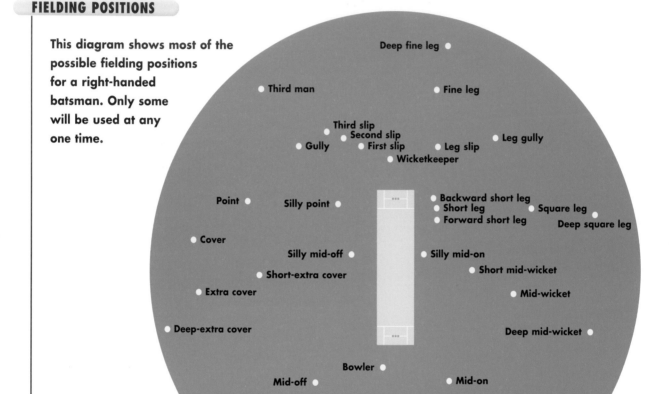

Deep fine leg

Third man   Fine leg

Third slip

Second slip   Leg gully

Gully   First slip   Leg slip

Wicketkeeper

Point   Silly point   Backward short leg

Short leg   Square leg

Forward short leg

Cover   Deep square leg

Silly mid-off   Silly mid-on

Short-extra cover   Short mid-wicket

Extra cover   Mid-wicket

Deep-extra cover   Deep mid-wicket

Bowler

Mid-off   Mid-on

Long on

Long off

WICKETKEEPER

Wicketkeeping is covered on pages 40 to 41. The keeper stands behind the stumps, further back if the bowler is quick and up to the stumps to a slower bowler.

SLIPS

Slips stand crouched on the off-side behind the wicket, with first slip next to, but just behind, the wicketkeeper. Second slip and third slip follow in the same direction. Many close catches are taken in the slip area, so reactions of these fielders have to be razor-sharp.

GULLY

This is another close catching position. The gully crouches just back of square on the off-side. Quick reactions are important in this position, as catching chances will be from forceful shots from the batsman.

POINT

Point is square of the wicket on the off-side. Fielders here will need to stop forceful shots played off the back foot, be ready to take catches and provide back-up. It's a very busy part of the cricket pitch to patrol.

COVER

The cover area runs from point to mid-off. As this is a large part of the off-side field, there are a few different positions here – extra cover, short-extra cover and deep-extra cover. It's a busy position and requires skill.

SILLY POINT

As the name suggests, crouching close to the batsman square of the wicket on the off-side is not a sensible place to field! This position is used when a spinner is bowling, and bat-pad catches may be given. Silly points wear protective equipment.

MID-OFF

This position is often taken up by the captain of the fielding team, so they can advise and encourage their bowlers. Their job is to cut off straight drives and prevent quick singles. Mid-off is normally about 25-30 yards (22-27 m) from the batsman, while silly mid-off is in close to the batsman for bat-pad chances.

MID-WICKET

Mid-wicket stands on the leg side, between square leg and mid-on. Run-saving is the main aim of this position, although top-edged pulls are likely to provide catching chances here, so stay on your toes.

SQUARE LEG

This position is square of the wicket on the leg side. Fielders here must be ready to take sharp catches and move in to cut off quick singles. Deep square leg is back on the boundary.

THIRD MAN

Third man stands behind the wicketkeeper on the off-side, usually 45 degrees to the wicket and near or on the boundary, and walks in as the bowler approaches the wicket. Anything that goes through the slip and gully area must be retrieved by the fielder standing here.

FINE LEG

Fine leg stands roughly between square leg and the wicketkeeper on the leg side. Although it's an important run-saving position, it is usually occupied by the bowler to give them a rest between overs.

EQUIPMENT

*F*or an organised game on a cricket pitch using a hard ball, you will need equipment including pads, gloves, wicketkeeping gloves and safety helmets.

SHIRT

Cricket shirts are normally white and made of cotton or a similar lightweight material. They can have either short or long sleeves. Sweaters can be worn over the shirt in cooler conditions.

BAT

Cricket bats are made of wood. A full-size bat must be no more than 38 inches (96 cm) in length and cannot exceed 4¼ inches (11 cm) at its widest part. Smaller size bats can be used by younger players. Cricket bats need to be looked after. They should be oiled and 'knocked in' before being used. Many players keep their bats inside a protective cover and they should never be stored when damp.

This end is called the toe.

KOOKABURRA · THE BEAST

This is called the shoulder.

BOOTS

These are white and usually made of a mixture of leather and plastic. They must be flexible and comfortable. Moulded or screw-in metal spikes are worn for outside games.
For indoor games, boots need to have a good grip. Specialist bowling boots feature greater ankle support, and batting boots feature extra protection for the toes.

BOX

A box must be worn by all male batsmen and wicketkeepers to protect the groin area.
It is a hard moulded plastic cup that is held in place by wearing support garments.

HELMET

Helmets must also be worn in organised games for younger players. Helmets are worn when batting, and when wicketkeepers are standing behind the stumps to a slower bowler. They are made of a hard but fairly lightweight material, and protect the top and sides of the head. They must be well-fitted and are secured by a strap under the chin. Helmets should be looked after and never thrown on the ground.

BATTING PADS

Batting pads offer protection to the ankles, shins and lower leg to just above the knee. They should be lightweight and comfortable. They are fastened with two or three Velcro strips or buckles at the back. Pads are different and offer different protection for right- and left-handed players.

BATTING GLOVES

These protect the fingers and thumb of the bottom hand. They are usually fastened at the wrist with Velcro, and should fit comfortably. Gloves are different for right- and left-handers.

TROUSERS

Cricket trousers are white and made of cotton or a similar lightweight material that does not limit movement. They should be washed after each game as they tend to become marked with grass stains.

WICKETKEEPING GLOVES

Wicketkeeping gloves protect the fingers, palms and top of the thumbs.
They are usually made of soft leather and must be flexible enough to allow the keeper to comfortably catch a ball one-handed. They should fit well and not be too tight. Cotton inner gloves are sometimes worn underneath.

BALL

A cricket ball is made of leather and should weigh 5½–5¾ ounces (155–163 g).
A stitched seam goes around the ball, fixing the two sides together.

BATTING – THE BASICS

*B*atting requires a solid technique. You need to be able to play attacking and defensive strokes off both the front and back foot. Concentrate on your shot selection. If you are a top-order batsman, remember you have a job to do for the team. Defend against good deliveries and look to score runs off loose bowling.

AT THE CREASE

When you arrive at the crease, ask the umpire at the bowler's end to help you take guard. This is a way of securing your position relative to the stumps. Many players will ask for a middle guard, where the bat is in line with middle stump. Others prefer a guard between middle and leg stumps. Stand further forward in the crease to a fast bowler, and further back to a slower bowler.

TAKING GUARD

When addressing the umpire, hold your bat up straight and call clearly for "Middle" or "Middle and leg" (also known as "Two"). The umpire will indicate whether your bat needs to be moved towards or slightly away from your body. Once you have the correct guard, mark the spot by tapping the ground lightly with your bat or creating a mark with your studs.

GRIP

Keep the top hand firm. The bottom hand can be slightly more relaxed. The top hand rests comfortably on the inside of the front thigh. Ask a coach or a senior player in your club to help you with your grip.

STANCE

STEP 1

Your feet should be about shoulder-width apart. Your back foot should be behind and parallel to the popping crease. Keep your weight on the balls of your feet, with your knees slightly bent.

STEP 2

Your head should be still, balanced and facing down the pitch.

Grip and stance are the same for left-handed batsmen.

SHOT SELECTION

What shot you use depends on the line, length and speed of the bowler's delivery. Move your feet to get back or forward depending on the shot selected. Play forward to a ball that is pitched up. Play back to a ball that is short of a length, giving yourself more time to execute a stroke.

THE BACKLIFT

The top hand controls the backlift which means the bat can be brought down in line with the ball.

Keep your hands close to the back hip so that the toe of the bat is around shoulder height.

THE WAGON WHEEL

The wagon wheel shows the direction in which specific shots are played by a right-handed batsman.

As a rough guide, it can help batsmen practice where to best position their shots.

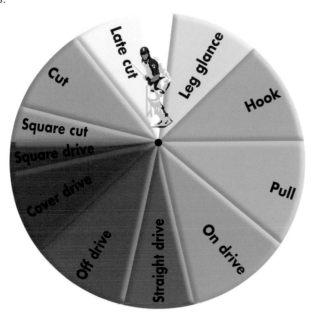

THE FORWARD PRESS

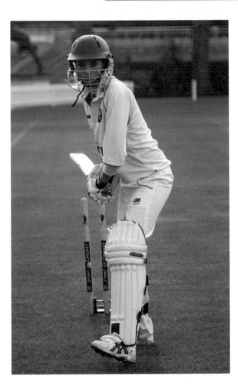

The forward press is a technique designed to assist foot movement.

The intention is to begin to transfer the weight onto the front foot just as the bowler is about to release the ball. It anticipates that the player will be playing forward. A half-step forward can be fully extended if the ball is pitched up. If the ball is short, the player is still able to move back.

TOP TIP
Settle, focus and take a good look at the field before you get into position to face the first ball.

FORWARD & BACKWARD DEFENCE

As a top-order batsman, you should be looking to score runs. But you can only score runs if you are at the crease. Building an innings is all about shot selection. If a ball is pitched at the stumps on a good length, defend. Keep your defence solid but relaxed, and hold the finished position, rather than following through.

FORWARD DEFENCE

Play the forward defensive shot to a delivery slightly short of a length that will hit the bat at bail height.

STEP 1

From the backlift, decide on the pitch of the ball.

STEP 2

Get to the pitch of the ball by transferring your weight onto the front foot. Bend your knee and make sure there is no gap between bat and pad.

STEP 3

Keep the bat as straight as possible – 'show the maker's name'. Let the ball come to you rather than pushing at it with a firm bottom hand.

STEP 4

Keep your front elbow high. Keep your bottom hand relaxed, allowing the bat to drop onto the ball. This helps to keep the ball down.

BACKWARD DEFENCE

Play the backward defensive shot to a delivery that is short of a length and bouncing in line with the stumps.

STEP 1

From the backlift, decide the ball is short and straight enough to play back.

STEP 2

Move your rear foot back and across the stumps.

STEP 3

Keep your head forward and over the ball. The weight of your body is on the back foot, which has moved backwards as far as possible.

STEP 4

Raise the front elbow, gripping the bat handle firmly with the top hand. Only the thumb and forefinger of the bottom hand should be in contact with the handle.

Keep the bat as straight as possible by keeping the front arm straight and high. The back arm should be tucked into the chest.

Try to stop the ball dead. Keep your hands relaxed to take the pace off the ball. This reduces the chance of being caught close to the wicket.

Always make sure you are wearing the correct equipment when you are batting against a hard ball. This includes pads, gloves, a box and helmet.

TOP TIP
Keep your eye on the ball! Top batsmen try to watch the ball so closely that they can see the maker's name.

DRIVING

*T*he drive is a scoring stroke that can be played off the front or back foot. It's an elegant shot, requiring balance and timing, rather than pure power. Most of the work is done by the top hand.

THE OFF DRIVE

The off drive can be played off the front foot to a ball that is slightly over-pitched and outside off stump.

STEP 1

From the backlift, decide the ball is full enough to drive.

STEP 2

Fix your eyes on the ball. Get your feet moving by leaning in with the front foot. From a high backlift, bring the full face of the bat through the line of the ball.

STEP 3

Your front foot should be level with the ball when it pitches. Your head should be level with or ahead of the front knee. Grip the bat firmly with your bottom hand as you make contact, accelerating through the ball.

STEP 4

The bottom arm should be fully extended in the follow-through, with your rear shoulder pulled under your chin.

The on drive can be played off the front foot into the leg side to a ball that is over-pitched on leg stump.

STEP 1

Lead with your head and shoulders, followed by the front foot, then the arms and bat.

STEP 2

Dip the front shoulder as the front foot moves towards the pitch of the ball.

THE ON DRIVE

STEP 3

Rotate your hips slightly as your hands lead a straight swing of the bat into a high follow-through.

THE STRAIGHT DRIVE

When played against fast bowling and with perfect timing, a checked straight drive can race to the boundary. It's a pretty good looking shot as well!

When playing the straight drive, lock the wrists instead of following through. This is a good way of ensuring that you do not swing across the line.

DRIVING OFF THE BACK FOOT

Drive off the back foot to a ball short of a length on or outside off stump. It's not advisable to play this shot on a pitch when the ball is keeping low.

The back foot drive is played with the head over the ball. The top hand controls the stroke, while the bottom hand punches through the ball to provide power.

TOP TIP
A lofted drive is a shot that is deliberately hit high into the air over the infielders. It's a useful stroke when fielders are positioned around the bat.

CUTTING, SWEEPING & GLANCING

Cuts, sweeps and glances are attacking shots and useful for finding the gaps in the field. Make sure you have played yourself in before attempting these shots. You'll need to be aware of how the pitch is playing, and whether the ball is swinging or moving off the seam.

THE CUT SHOT

The cut shot is played to a ball that is short and wide. Play it when you have plenty of time to sight the ball and get your feet into position.

STEP 1

Move back and across. The bottom hand controls the cut shot, and the hands and arms throw the bat into the stroke.

STEP 2

Transfer the weight fully onto the back foot. Play the ball at arm's length, square of you, or behind you. The end of the bat should dip slightly, to keep the ball down. Complete the shot with a long follow-through of the arms.

THE SWEEP SHOT

The sweep is a difficult shot to play as it's a cross-batted forward stroke. Both legs are bent so that the ball can be literally swept away to the leg side with the bat almost horizontal to the pitch.

When playing the sweep shot, make sure that the ball hits the pad if you fail to make contact.

STEP 1

Lean towards the line of the ball. Place your front leg in line with the ball. Bend the front knee and collapse the back leg.

STEP 2

Stretch the arms to hit the ball in front of the pad. The ball should be struck when close to the ground, from a crouching position.

STEP 3

Both shoulders face down the pitch. Roll the wrists as you strike the ball, keeping it down and guiding it round the corner behind square leg.

The leg glance is a delicate shot, often announced by commentators as a 'tickle round the corner'.

STEP 1

The leg glance can be played off the back foot. Your initial movements are the same as the backward defensive. But instead of dead-batting the ball in front of the wicket, get inside the line of the ball.

STEP 2

Play the ball in front of the body, turning the bat face slightly towards leg as you make contact. The bat makes minimal impact, turning the ball round the corner rather than forcing it. The ball should hit the front pad if you fail to make contact.

The glance can be played off the front foot in the same way but with the feet further forward.

COMING DOWN THE WICKET

Once you have got your eye in and had a good look at a slower bowler, you can take a couple of quick steps down the wicket as the ball is about to be released.

STEP 1

Keep your body side-on with your head straight and balanced.

STEP 3

Get your front foot to the pitch of the ball. You can drop the bat on the ball at the last minute if it is bowled faster and flatter.

STEP 2

The most nimble-footed players literally skip down the wicket.

STEP 4

The intention is to hit the ball on the full, driving it over or through the infield.

TOP TIP

Don't play the leg glance outside the line of the body and use the wrists to flick the ball. Too fine a glance to a fast delivery may result in a catch to the wicketkeeper.

PULLING & HOOKING

Pulling and hooking are attacking shots against fast, short-pitched bowling. These are difficult and risky shots, requiring very quick footwork, so try to keep your eye on the ball at all times.

THE PULL

The pull is played to a short-pitched delivery. The line of the ball does not matter too much.

STEP 1

From the backlift, your head, shoulders and back foot begin to move back and across.

STEP 2

The back foot pivots and the body opens so that you are facing down the pitch when you make contact. The ball should be hit around waist height.

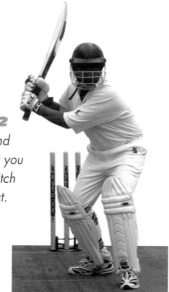

STEP 3

Try to play the ball to square leg, hitting down and keeping the head still. Do not allow your head to fall back, as this will pull your body back. This results in a half-hit stroke off the top edge of the bat.

THE HOOK

This is one of the most difficult shots to play. Even top players have difficulty in controlling the hook shot. It's a risky shot as a hook played to a ball that is delivered more quickly may result in a top-edged catch on the boundary.

STEP 1

Position yourself as for the pull shot.

STEP 2

Move the head and back foot quickly inside the line of the ball. The ball is directed towards or backwards of square leg.

STEP 3

Twist the upper body round in the follow-through.

It may be too risky to attempt to play a short, quick delivery on the stumps. Avoid bouncers by ducking inside or swaying outside the line of the ball, allowing it to pass through to the wicketkeeper.

Duck across and inside a bouncer on the leg side.

Do not turn your chest and arms round to duck under the ball. This may cause the bat to wave around in the air, increasing the chance of a catch behind.

Try to stay sideways on, swaying back and pulling the head away from a middle-stump bouncer.

PLAYING THE FULL TOSS TO LEG

A full toss is a 'gift ball', but don't get over-confident. Keep your eye on the ball and play it correctly – don't slog.

STEP 1
From the backlift, decide you are going to play a full toss at waist height.

STEP 2
Try to pull the ball, rolling the wrists to keep the ball down.

STEP 3
Play the ball square of the wicket. A low full toss should be played with a straight bat.

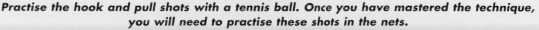

TOP TIP
Practise the hook and pull shots with a tennis ball. Once you have mastered the technique, you will need to practise these shots in the nets.

CALLING & RUNNING

*C*alling and running between the wickets are crucial parts of batting. Be positive and aim to put pressure on the fielding side, but don't take unnecessary risks. Know when it is your call and when to listen to your batting partner. Try to avoid run-outs by clear and decisive calling.

BACKING UP

It's difficult to sprint down the pitch for a run from a standing position.
At the non-striker's end, you should be on the move as the bowler approaches the wicket.

STEP 1
At the non-striker's end, back up by taking a step forwards, so that you are moving out of the crease as the bowler is about to deliver the ball.

STEP 2
Watch the other batsman and keep your eye on the ball until after it has been hit. You may need to duck out of the way of a hard-hit straight drive.

CALLING

A batsman calls for a run if the ball is hit in front of the wicket. When the ball is hit behind and the batsman's view is obscured, the non-striker calls. The three calls are "Yes", "Wait" or "No". Positive and early calling are the key to good running between the wickets. If there is any initial doubt, the call should be "Wait".

A non-striker raises a hand clearly when calling "No".

RUNNING HARD

One of the most successful features of the great Australian sides of recent years has been their running between the wickets. The latest in a long line of hard runners is Michael Clarke. You never see him gently jogging to the non-striker's end!

Always run hard, particularly on the first run. Show the fielding side that you mean business.

TURNING FOR A SECOND

As you reach the popping crease, look up to see where the ball and fielder are before calling for a second run.

Make sure you ground your bat behind the crease before you turn.

GROUNDING YOUR BAT

Run your bat along the ground as you reach the crease.

It's important that the bat makes contact with the ground to avoid being run out.

 TOP TIP
Run hard to turn a dead ball into a single or a single into a two. Putting pressure on fielders may even result in fumbles and overthrows.

BATTING FITNESS & TRAINING

Make sure you train properly and sensibly. Warm up before a batting session in the nets and before you go to the wicket. Use net sessions to work on your weaknesses, perhaps with a bowling machine under the supervision of a coach. Make sure you warm down properly at the end of any net training session.

General warm-up and stretching before a batting session.

BATTING COACHING

Seek advice from a coach or senior player.

Ask them to watch you bat in the nets and to consider ways in which you might improve a particular aspect of your game.

NET PRACTICE

Use your net sessions to practise shots around the wicket. Use the wagon wheel on page 11.

Batting practice in the nets can sometimes be with throws half-way down the pitch or a bowling machine (left).

LAW 36 – LBW EXPLAINED

L BW appeals happen within the space of a few seconds. During that time, the umpire has to consider a number of factors before reaching a decision.

THE LAW

A batsman is judged out LBW if he or she prevents the ball hitting the wicket with any part of the body, not just the leg. A batsman attempting to play the ball is out if the ball:

- *pitches in a straight line between the two sets of stumps*
- *pitches on the off side, but hits the batsman in a line between the wickets*
- *hits the batsman on the full and would have pitched in a straight line between the two sets of stumps.*

A batsman cannot be out if the ball would not have hit the wicket.

MAKING A DECISION

The umpire will consider an LBW decision if they believe the ball would have hit the stumps had its path not been obstructed by the batsman's pads or body. But there are a number of other factors to be considered.

PITCHING OUTSIDE LEG

The first thing an umpire must consider before making a decision is: did the ball pitch outside leg stump? If the ball lands outside the line of leg stump, the batsman cannot be given out, even if the ball would have gone on to hit the stumps.

OTHER FACTORS

In the deliveries shown left, the ball has pitched on the stumps and strikes the batsman on the pads in front of the wicket. As the ball has not pitched outside the line of leg stump and has not struck the batsman outside the line of off stump, the umpire should give the batsman out. However, they must also consider other factors:

- *The height of the ball's bounce and the point at which the ball hit the pad (red arrow). If the umpire decides the ball may have gone over the stumps, the batsman is given not out.*
- *The swing or spin of the ball (blue arrow). If the ball would have swung or spun too much and missed the stumps, the batsman is given not out.*

line of stumps

OUT!

If batsman plays a no stroke

OUT!

PLAYING NO STROKE – OUT

Finally, the umpire must decide whether the batsman is making a genuine attempt to play a stroke. If the batsman makes no attempt to play the ball, they may be given out even if the ball hits the pad outside the line of off stump and provided the umpire feels the ball would go on to hit the stumps.

BOWLING – THE BASICS

There are four elements of bowling: run-up, approach to the wicket, delivery and follow-through. Whether fast, medium-paced or slow, bowlers should aim to deliver the ball with a smooth repeatable action from a set run-up. The pace of your bowling may change as you develop. A young medium-paced bowler may become a fast bowler; or switch to slow bowling.

GRIP

The standard grip for a medium-paced bowler is with fingers held either side of a straight seam.

APPROACH TO THE WICKET

A smooth approach to the wicket is essential. Try to stay close to the stumps.

RUN-UP

Try to develop an even-paced, relaxed and balanced run-up.

TOP TIP

The ideal length for a bowler is where the batsman is unsure whether to play forward or back.

DELIVERY

STEP 1

As you raise the front arm, pull the ball close to your chin with your head looking behind a high front arm.

STEP 2

As your back foot lands on the pitch, keep your body upright. Your back leg should remain stable and support the body while the front foot should be slightly raised.

STEP 3

Your front foot should be pointing to the batsman as it lands. The leg is braced and ready to take the full impact of the delivery.

STEP 4

The bowling arm comes over to release the ball at maximum height. At the moment of delivery, the fingers should be behind the ball, with the wrist stiff and straight. This helps to control accuracy and swing.

FOLLOW-THROUGH

A full follow-through is essential for all bowlers, whether fast or slow. *Move away from the pitch as you follow through. A bowler is not allowed to run on the pitch more than four feet past the bowling crease and within one foot of the middle stump.*

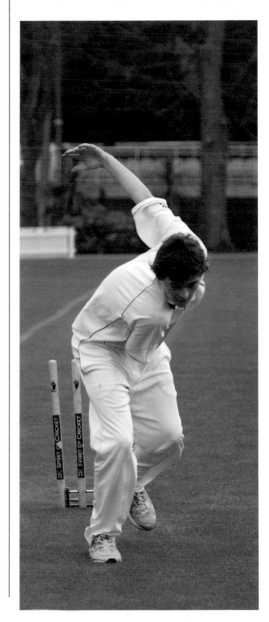

TOP TIP

Don't allow a batsman to settle. Vary your deliveries and identify a batsman's strengths and weaknesses in order to plan an over that keeps them guessing.

FAST BOWLING

If you are a fast bowler, you are likely to open the bowling. The first couple of overs in an innings sets the tone for the fielding side. You'll need to be accurate as you are bowling against the best batsmen in the opposing team. Set your field carefully before your first ball. Mark out your run-up and bowl a couple of practice balls to one of your team-mates. Once the batsman is ready and the umpire has called "Play", you can begin your first over.

OVER & ROUND THE WICKET

The umpire will ask you whether you intend to bowl over or round the wicket before you begin your first over.

When going round the wicket (above), a bowler approaches to the right of the stumps, so that the ball is angled across the pitch. This can unsettle a right-handed batsman. It's also a useful tactic against left-handers.

Most right-arm fast bowlers bowl over the wicket (right). In this case, the bowler approaches to the left of the wicket as he or she faces it.

1

2

3

SIDE-ON DELIVERY

Most fast bowlers deliver the ball with a side-on action, looking over the front shoulder.

CHEST-ON DELIVERY

SLOWER BALL

Some fast bowlers, such as Andrew Flintoff, are more front-on when releasing the ball.

Neither action is wrong, but a mixture of front and side-on can put stress on the spine. Make sure that you get your action checked out by a bowling coach. 'Keep the hips and shoulders in line and you'll be fine. Twist the back and it will crack' is a favourite saying of many coaches.

Once you have worked up a good pace, you can surprise a batsman by delivering a slower ball.

Many fast bowlers use a grip in which the fingers are split apart either side of the ball. You'll need to perfect this type of slower ball in training before you attempt it in a match.

Your first delivery should be a slower loosener. Build up towards full pace in your first few balls.

TOP TIP
Never make the mistake of substituting speed for accuracy.

SWING & SEAM BOWLING

A heavy atmosphere with low cloud cover on match day helps the ball to swing in the air. Pitch conditions may affect the movement of the ball as the seam hits the wicket. Shine on the ball is also important. Swing and seam bowlers use grips and bowling actions to make the most of these conditions.

SHINING THE BALL

Adding shine to the ball on one side can make the ball swing through the air. This makes the line more difficult for the batsmen to judge.

INSWINGER

The inswinger moves in the air towards the batsman's leg side. It should be bowled outside off stump so that it swings into the wicket.

To bowl an inswinger to a right-handed batsman, the ball is held so that the shiny side (shown here by the white side of the ball) points to the off side, away from the wicket. The ball is held with the fingers close together. The vertical seam points towards fine leg.

STEP 1

To deliver an inswinger, keep close to the stumps at the point of delivery.

STEP 2

The ball is pushed towards the off stump from a slightly open-chested position.

OUTSWINGER

The outswinger moves in the air away from the batsman towards the slips. It should be aimed at middle and off stump, so that the batsman is forced to play at it, edging to the keeper or slips as the ball deviates.

To swing the ball away from the batsman, the ball is held so that the shiny side (shown here as the white side of the ball) is the inner side of the ball, pointing in the direction of the wicket. The fingers are placed either side of the seam. The vertical seam should point towards the slips. Pitch the ball up to a batsman when bowling an outswinger.

An off-cutter will move off the pitch towards the right-handed batsman.

To bowl an off-cutter, the fingers cut across the ball. At the moment of delivery, the seam is pulled down by the first finger in a clockwise direction. For a swing bowler, it's a great delivery as it forces the batsman to play at slightly wider outswingers.

To produce movement off the pitch, seam bowlers use the basic bowling grip (see page 24). A good seam bowler relies on accuracy, a firm wrist at the point of delivery, and variations in pace.

Indoor games are played according to a set of rules that keep the games short and fast-paced. Batsmen will look to score runs off every ball, so bowling accuracy is essential.

TOP TIP
Fast and medium-pace bowlers should be able to bowl a good yorker right up in the block-hole. This is a very difficult ball for a batsman to play if it is swinging in.

OFF-SPIN BOWLING

Off-spin bowlers use grip, bowling action, and helpful pitch conditions to turn the ball off the wicket and into the right-handed batsman after it has pitched. Accurate spin bowling with a deep-set field can be used as a defensive tactic by the fielding team. It can be used as an attacking tactic on a pitch where the ball is spinning and close catchers are crowded around the batsman.

GRIP

The ball is gripped with the tips of the first and second fingers placed on the seam.

The first finger is the main spinning finger. The thumb plays no part in spinning the ball. The ball should be directed outside off stump so that it moves in towards the batsman.

A good off-spinner will use clever variations in pace and flight to unsettle batsmen.

DELIVERY

STEP 1

As the hand is brought up, the wrist and fingers twist clockwise and carry on doing so until after the ball has left the hand.

STEP 2

The delivery stride is slightly across the crease.

STEP 4

The front leg is braced as the bowler releases the ball. The first two fingers give the ball a good 'rip' as it is released. A full follow-through whips the bowling arm across the body.

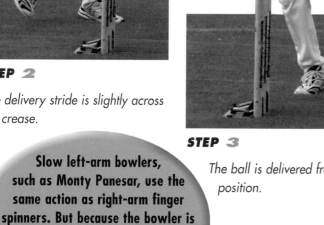

Slow left-arm bowlers, such as Monty Panesar, use the same action as right-arm finger spinners. But because the bowler is left-handed, the ball will spin away from a right-handed batsman towards the slips.

STEP 3

The ball is delivered from a high position.

The off-spinner turns from outside off stump in towards the batsman. The very best off-spinner can bowl a ball that appears to be heavily spun but does not spin at all, instead drifting away from the right-handed batsman.

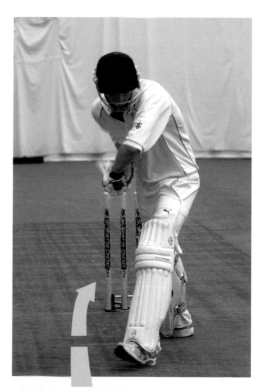

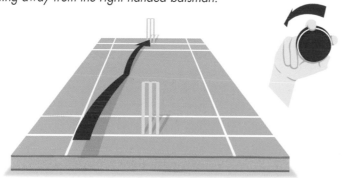

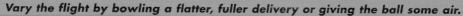

TOP TIP
Vary the flight by bowling a flatter, fuller delivery or giving the ball some air.

LEG-SPIN BOWLING

The leg-spinner moves from leg to off, away from the batsman, after it has pitched. Leg-spin bowling used to be considered a defensive option. Shane Warne and Muttiah Muralitharan have made leg-spin bowling a form of all-out attack. With fielders crowding round the bat, these great 'leggies' approach the wicket and explode into action.

GRID

The ball is gripped so that it rests on the base of the thumb.

The first and second fingers hold the top of the ball along the seam. Spin is imparted by the wrist as the ball is delivered.

STEP 2

As the arm is brought up to the delivery position, the hand is cocked inwards (towards the front of the wrist).

DELIVERY

STEP 1

At the bottom of the bowling action, the wrist is bent forward with the fingers pointing towards the opposite wicket.

STEP 3

As the ball is released, the wrist flips the fingers forwards, twisting the ball in an anti-clockwise direction. As the ball is flipped out of the hand, the thumb and fingers move across the seam, dragging it in the same direction.

STEP 4

Move away from the pitch as you follow through after releasing the ball. Keep looking down the pitch towards the batsman and be ready for a return catch.

The googly is an off-spinner delivered with a leg-spinning action.

Each leg-spin bowler has their own type of delivery. The important thing is to practise so that your leg-spinner and googly look almost identical.

Googlies are delivered with the ball travelling over the fingers and the back of the hand, or by releasing the ball from the side of the hand.

Develop two actions for the googly, the first obviously different from the second. A batsman who thinks they have 'picked' your googly by recognising the different action will play the second 'disguised' googly action as a leg-spinner.

The leg-spinner turns off the pitch and away from a right-handed batsman to the off side.

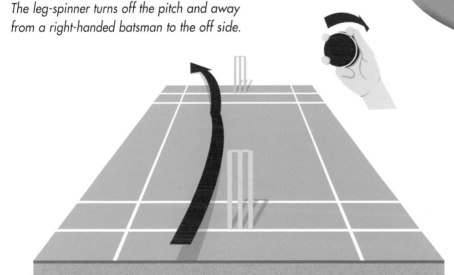

TOP TIP
The top spinner is delivered with the same grip and spin as the leg-spinner. The ball is over-spun towards the batsman, so that it gathers pace as it bounces off the pitch.

BOWLING FITNESS & TRAINING

Stretching exercises before bowling help to prevent injury. Make sure you warm up and warm down at the beginning and end of a net session.

WARMING UP

Bowling exercises should stretch the shoulders and lower back.

Over-bowling can lead to injury. Make sure you use short, focused net sessions to improve your bowling. The number of overs you are permitted to bowl in a match will probably be limited.

IN THE NETS

You can work on line and length by bowling at a set of stumps, or one stump, in a net. During net sessions, you are not only working to improve your own technique, but also to help your batting team-mates.

Net sessions should be well organised, with bowlers waiting at the back of the net taking turns to bowl. Don't walk into the net when you are not bowling, and keep your eye on the ball at all times.

BOWLING COACHING

Always be ready to listen to the advice of players and coaches who are willing to help you improve your game.

THE CORRIDOR OF UNCERTAINTY

Renowned cricket commentator Geoff Boycott often uses the phrase 'the corridor of uncertainty' to describe the ideal area to bowl at a batsman.

This is an imaginary channel around and just outside the off-stump. The batsman is unsure whether to play or leave the ball. Bowling consistently in this area builds pressure on a batsman. This will increase your chances of taking a wicket.

Most batsmen like the ball wide outside off stump or on leg stump, so try not to bowl in these areas.

If the ball lands between the two red lines, it could either bounce up and deceive them, given them out LBW, or be a playable shot resulting in runs.

BAD LINE

GOOD LINE

BAD LINE

TOP TIP
Fielding practices before the start of a game help to bring a side together and are a good way for the whole team to warm up.

FIELDING – THE BASICS

Fielders prevent runs by retrieving a ball along the ground and returning it accurately to the wicket. They help take wickets by catching the ball or assisting in a run-out. Players with quick reactions tend to field close to the bat. Fast, agile players will field on the edge of the square, but outfielders must also be able to catch, retrieve and throw accurately.

STOPPING THE BALL

The 'long barrier' is not very fashionable today, but it remains the safest way to field a ball along the ground.

If you are playing on an uneven surface, it is probably best to resort to this 'old-school' method of stopping the ball.

STEP 1

Move towards the ball, bending down and sideways as you reach it.

STEP 2

For a right-hander, bend the right knee and let the left leg trail along the ground. The legs should form a barrier with no gap. Field the ball with both hands. Your legs are a solid second line of defence should you fail to stop the ball cleanly with your hands.

You can also field the ball by running towards it and reaching down in front of your feet.

This is not as safe as the long barrier but allows you to make a return throw to the wicket more quickly.

THROWING

Once you have stopped the ball, you should get into position to throw it back to the wicket as quickly as possible.

Make sure you are balanced, and take aim with the non-throwing arm. Release the ball with a flat (or over-arm) action.

When fielding close to the wicket, stay on your toes to stop the batsmen from taking quick singles. Always be ready to seize a run out opportunity.

CATCHING

A ball at above chest height should be caught with the hands together and pointing up.

Catches win matches. All top players practise their catching as much as batting and bowling.

Point your hands sideways or down for catches below waist height.

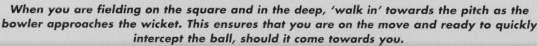

TOP TIP

When you are fielding on the square and in the deep, 'walk in' towards the pitch as the bowler approaches the wicket. This ensures that you are on the move and ready to quickly intercept the ball, should it come towards you.

CLOSE TO THE WICKET

Next time you are watching a live game or one on TV, try to watch the top-class infielders as the bowler approaches the crease. Most will be stooped forward with bent knees, and hands cupped in front of them.

CROUCHING POSITION

This is the textbook position for a close catcher such as a slip or gully fielder.

You should be still and looking at the batsman, particularly if you are in front of the wicket and close in.

CATCHING

Catches close to the wicket, for example in the slips, come at you very fast.

Let the ball come to you and try to take it with relaxed, 'soft' hands. This will increase the likelihood of catching the ball and prevents injury.

Keep your body balanced and your eyes on the ball as you take a catch to your left or right.

Infielders should move quickly towards a well-struck ball, aiming to intercept it before the batsmen have set off for a run.

STEP 1

Pick up the ball with both hands in front of the right foot for a right-handed throw.

STEP 2

Bend and turn the body sideways for the throw.

STEP 3

Release the ball with a flat (or over-arm) action.

BACKING UP

If you are fielding in close, be ready to back up a bowler or wicketkeeper by standing behind the stumps to receive a throw from the outfield.

PRACTICE

Catching practice is as important as bowling or batting practice.

PICK-UP & THROW

Fielders close to the wicket will often have the opportunity of running out a batsman at close range.

The one-handed pick-up and accurate underarm throw is the quickest way of retrieving and releasing the ball.

STEP 1

The pick-up and throw is achieved by running at the ball face-on.

STEP 2

The ball is intercepted and released with one hand. Release the ball early towards the target.

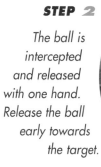

STEP 3

The palm of the hand follows through on a direct path for as long as possible. Watch Andrew Symonds fielding at cover-point for a lightning-fast demonstration.

TOP TIP
Good cover-point and mid-wicket fielders can dominate batsmen, stopping runs and building pressure.

WICKETKEEPING – THE BASICS

The wicketkeeper has obvious responsibilities. Catches behind, stumpings and run-outs require agility, co-ordination and quick thinking. But a good keeper can also pass on information to the captain and bowlers. He or she is also likely to provide encouragement to the bowlers and other members of the team.

STANDING UP

Position yourself behind the off stump so that your view of the ball is not obscured by the batsman. You should crouch down with gloves held palm up in front of you.

To a slow bowler, you should feel comfortable standing up to the wicket.

TAKING A CATCH

Tidy wicketkeeping that demonstrates clean catching and an awareness of stumping opportunities keeps batsmen 'honest'. It sets the tone for the fielding performance and keeps the game going at a good pace. Make sure your glovework is safe and get the ball back to the bowler at a catchable height, using other fielders if necessary.

Taking a catch behind the stumps requires concentration. But you also need to be relaxed, letting the ball come to you. Watch the ball all the way into the gloves.

STEP 1

Relax and let the hands 'give'. Try to avoid snatching or grabbing at the ball.

STEP 2

Try to take the ball with the arms as straight as possible.

The fingers should be pointing up or down, but never at the ball.

Once a scoring stroke has been made, you need to run to the wicket as quickly as possible and be ready for a return throw from a fielder.

STEP 1

Get behind or over the stumps. Be aware of where both batsmen are. Call to the fielder to indicate which end they should throw the ball to. Be ready to move if the throw is inaccurate.

STEP 2

Catch the ball with both hands and move it on to the stumps in a smooth continuous movement.

You may need to take the ball one-handed if the throw is inaccurate.

If you fail to catch the ball, you'll need to retrieve it.

STEP 1

Discard the glove from your throwing hand as you run to retrieve the ball.

STEP 2

One of your team-mates should be ready to receive your throw over the stumps.

TOP TIP
Stay in the crouching position for as long as possible. A common fault among keepers is to get up too early.

OUT!

*T*here are a number of ways in which a batsman can be dismissed; each is covered in the laws of the game. Here is a summary:

BEING CAUGHT

The most common way for a batsman to be dismissed is being caught by a fielder. When a player in the fielding side catches the ball directly off the bat, before it has hit the ground, the batsman is out. The ball does not have to come directly off the bat – it can deflect from the pad on to the bat or from the bat on to the pad, but the fielder must take the ball cleanly above the ground.
A batsman can not be given out if they are caught off a no ball.

If a bowler takes a catch off their own bowling, the batsman is out – caught and bowled. When a wicketkeeper takes the catch, the batsman is out – caught behind.

If the ball hits the batsman below the wrist, then they are caught out so long as their hand is in contact with the bat.

If a fielder catches the ball as it crosses the boundary, the batsman is out as long as the fielder does not touch the boundary or the ground beyond it. His or her feet must remain inside the boundary, though their hands may be over it.

BOWLED

When a bowler manages to get the ball past the bat and knocks off the bails, the batsman is bowled out. A batsman is bowled out if he or she accidentally deflects the ball onto the stumps off the bat or pad.

> **REMEMBER:**
> **You cannot be bowled off a no-ball.**

HITTING THE BALL TWICE

A batsman can be given out for hitting the ball twice if the second strike is deliberate. The only exceptions to this rule allow a batsman to hit the ball to stop it from rolling back on to the stumps, or to return the ball to the fielding team with permission.

A batsman is not allowed to hit the ball a second time to prevent a catch, and is also out if in hitting the ball a second time to protect the wicket, a catch is prevented.

HIT WICKET

This dismissal happens when the batsman hits the stumps with the bat or any part of the body while playing a shot or avoiding a delivery. It does happen in cricket played at all levels, so try to stay balanced when you play a shot.

STUMPED

A stumping happens when the wicketkeeper collects the ball and knocks off the bails before the batsman gets their bat or any part of their body grounded behind the batting crease. The batsman must have something in contact with the ground behind the crease – touching the batting crease with the bat or heel of the foot is out.

If a batsman thinks the ball will roll back onto the stumps after playing a shot, they are allowed to knock the ball away with the bat, feet or pads, but not the hands. You cannot be stumped off a no-ball, but you can be run-out stumped if the umpire has called the ball wide.

HANDLING THE BALL

Batsmen are not allowed to deflect the ball with their hands. You rarely see this type of dismissal in a game, but it can happen. The only exception to this law is when a batsman picks the ball up off the pitch and passes it back to a fielder. Make sure you tell the fielding side you are about to do this!

OBSTRUCTING THE FIELD

Try to avoid fielders when you are running between the wickets to prevent injures, and avoid being given out for obstructing the field!

The umpire can give a batsman out if they have deliberately got in the way of a fielder who is about to take a catch or attempt a run out. It is considered bad sportsmanship and so this very uncommon method of dismissal is hardly ever seen in junior, club or international cricket.

RUN OUT

A run out is when the batsmen are running between the wickets and fall short of the batting crease when the stumps are broken by the fielding team. To avoid this, the batsman must have some part of their bat or body grounded beyond the crease – on the line is out. This is why it is so important to run the bat along the ground with an outstretched arm in front of you as you reach the crease.

Even in Test matches, run outs often occur as teams focus on getting runs quickly. Run out decisions are tricky for umpires because they happen so fast. Umpires can choose to refer decisions to the third umpire, who will watch video replays before making a decision.

TIMED OUT

When a batting side loses a wicket, the next batsman must be at the crease to face the next ball within three minutes of the wicket falling. This rarely happens in a game and is considered to be bad sportsmanship, but if you are the next player in, make sure you are ready to take the field as soon as a wicket falls.

 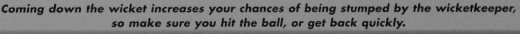

TOP TIP
Coming down the wicket increases your chances of being stumped by the wicketkeeper, so make sure you hit the ball, or get back quickly.

DIET & MENTAL ATTITUDE

You can give yourself more energy and stamina on the pitch by eating and drinking the right foods before, during and after a game. Above all, make sure you take in plenty of fluid during a game played on a hot day.

DIET

This is the recommended intake for a balanced and healthy diet, which is essential for top cricketers.

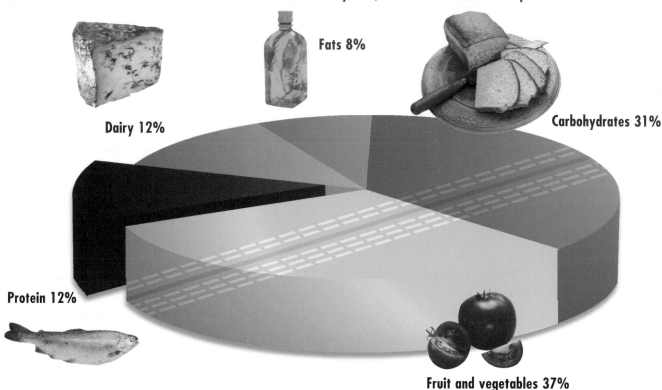

Fats 8%

Dairy 12%

Carbohydrates 31%

Protein 12%

Fruit and vegetables 37%

BEFORE THE GAME

To produce maximum energy before a game or training, you should eat a high carbohydrate meal not less than one hour beforehand. Low fat pasta or rice meals (with no creamy sauce) are ideal.

Between innings, boost your carbohydrate levels with fast-digesting snacks, such as bananas or dried fruit.

It is crucial to drink plenty of liquid before a game. Try to avoid fizzy or sugary drinks. Water or isotonic sports drinks consumed before play and during drink breaks will prevent dehydration during a game.

ENERGY BOOSTERS

When you are playing cricket and participating in net sessions, cut down on fatty foods and eat plenty of carbohydrates. Protein is necessary for the growth and repair of the body, so try to choose low fat sources, such lean meat, or fish.

MENTAL ATTITUDE

As well as preparing the body, it is also important to prepare the mind for a cricket match.

Be confident when you are going out to bat and stay alert at all times in the field. Listen to and support your captain. Play to win, but play fairly.

MENTAL PREPARATION

Before a game, focus your mind on the tasks ahead and visualise certain match situations and how you would deal with them.
If you are a batsman, plan to build an innings. If you are bowler, make sure you are warmed-up and focused on your line and length.

CAPTAINCY

If you are captaining a side, inspect the pitch and consider the playing conditions. Talk to your coach and decide whether you wish to bat or field first if you win the toss. Work out your batting order well in advance of the start of the game.
Keep your side organised by taking the field as a team. Make sure your fielders are in the correct position and encourage your bowlers during the course of the innings.

YOUR COACH

Cricket coaches or senior players can provide tips to help you improve your game. Respect their experience, ask them questions and listen carefully to their advice.

You may get the opportunity to play with older players. Watch the senior club players during a game and try to learn more about your own game by studying their techniques.

THE SPIRIT OF THE GAME
Respect the spirit as well as the laws of the game. Accept all umpiring decisions, clap incoming batsmen and never resort to verbal abuse or sledging. Congratulate your team-mates and opponents at the end of a match. Above all, enjoy your cricket.

HOW THE FAMOUS DO IT

Most people play cricket for fun but a few lucky individuals are professionals who travel the world playing the game AND getting paid for it. It takes hard work, dedication and hours of fitness training and net practise to make it to the top.

TYPICAL TEST MATCH DAY

7.00	Wake up
7.30	Breakfast
8.30	Report to ground
9.15	Player and coach consultations
9.30	Fitness treatment or short net session
10.00	Organised warm-up sessions on the field
10.30	Start of play
1.00	Lunch break
1.40	Start of afternoon session
4.00	Tea
6.00	Close of play
6.30	Warm-down
7.00	Press conference or post-match interviews
7.30	Dinner
8.30	Study video of day's play with coach
10.30	Bed

SPORTSMANSHIP

Sportsmanship is an important part of the spirit of cricket.

There is no better illustration of this than in Andrew Flintoff's famous consolation of Brett Lee at the end of the historic third test between England and Australia in 2005.

LIFE ON TOUR

International cricketers now play for most of the year. During the summer months, England players must keep themselves fit and in form to play up to five home test matches, as well as one-day internationals and Twenty20 fixtures. They will also occasionally represent their county.

At the end of the domestic season, players may be asked to participate in overseas tours representing their country. Squad players attend overseas training academies. Top-level cricket can involve long periods away from friends and family, which can lead to homesickness. A good team spirit and positive mental attitude will help to overcome this.

MEDIA WORK

International players are often required to do interviews for television, particularly the sports TV channels and radio.

Captains will be expected to take part in brief TV interviews during presentation ceremonies at the end of the game. This honour also goes to those who are fortunate enough to win Player-of-the-Match awards. In addition, players may be required to attend post-match press conferences with journalists, like Ricky Ponting, captain of Australia (left).

MONEY

Cricket's top players can earn huge sums of money. A centrally contracted England player may be paid as much as £300,000 each year.

In addition, player's agents are able to negotiate deals that earn a player extra money by endorsing or promoting certain products. Some players make well-paid book deals with publishers for their autobiographies.

GLOSSARY

BOUNCER *A short, fast delivery that bounces at a batsman at chest height.*

BLOCK-HOLE *Where the toe end of the bat meets the ground.*

BYES *Runs resulting from a ball that passes the batsman and is not collected cleanly by the wicketkeeper.*

DUCK *A score of zero.*

FULL TOSS *A ball that does not bounce.*

KNOCKED IN *A way of toughening a cricket bat by tapping or knocking it with a special mallet.*

LEG BYES *Runs resulting from a ball that hits a batsman's pad and is not collected cleanly by the wicketkeeper.*

LEG SIDE / ON SIDE *The side of the wicket behind a sideways facing batsman.*

MAIDEN *An over in which no runs attributable to the bowler are scored.*

NO BALL *A foul ball, bowled when a bowler oversteps the crease or bowls a full-toss at above shoulder height.*

OFF SIDE *The side of the wicket in front of a sideways facing batsman.*

OVER *A sequence of six balls bowled by a bowler from one end of the pitch.*

OVER-PITCHED *A ball that bounces just in front of a batsman standing in the crease that can be easily driven.*

OVER-THROWS *A throw at the wicket by a fielder that is not collected by an infielder resulting in extra runs.*

RUNNER *A player who is called by an injured batsman to run on their behalf. The runner wears full batting equipment and stands at square leg or the non-striker's end.*

RUN RATE *The average number of runs scored per over. This is used to measure a side's progress in a limited overs game.*

SLEDGING *Verbally abusing a batsman to unsettle them. It is not within the spirit of the game.*

WIDE *A ball that is too wide for a batsman to play at.*

YORKER *A ball that jams into the ground at the toe end of the bat.*

LISTINGS

The International Cricket Council
Al Thuraya Tower 1, 11th floor
Dubai Media City, Dubai, United Arab Emirates
Tel: +971 4 368 8088   Fax: +971 4 368 8080
Website: www.icc-cricket.com

The England and Wales Cricket Board
Lord's Cricket Ground, London NW8 8QZ
Tel: +44 (0)20 7432 1200   Fax: +44 (0)20 7286 5583
Website: www.ecb.co.uk

Cricket News
Latest cricket scores and news from fixtures around the world.
Website www.cricinfo.com

Lord's Cricket Ground
Marylebone Cricket Club, Lord's Cricket Ground
St John's Wood, London NW8 8QN
Tel:+44 (0)20 7616 8500
Website: www.lords.org